Unto Us a Child Is Born

THE DEVELOPMENT OF THE UNBORN CHILD IN THE FEASTS OF THE LORD

Michael D. Hodge

Copyright © 1983, 1995, 2012 Michael D. Hodge. All rights reserved

Unless otherwise noted, all scripture is from the New King James Version, Copyright 1982, Thomas Nelson, Inc. All rights reserved. Database © 2004 WORD*search* Corp.

Scripture designated (KJV) is from the King James Version.

Scripture designated (NASB) is from the New American Standard Bible (1995 Update). Copyright © 1981, 1998 THE LOCKMAN FOUNDATION, A Corporation Not for Profit, La Habra, California. All Rights Reserved. International Copyright Secured.

Table of Contents

Preface. i

Introduction. iii

Chapter 1
    The New Birth. 1

Chapter 2
    Passover. 9

Chapter 3
    The Feast of Unleavened Bread. 13

Chapter 4
    The Wave Sheaf Offering. 17

Chapter 5
    Pentecost. 23

Chapter 6
    The Feast of Trumpets. 27

Chapter 7
    The Day of Atonement. 31

Chapter 8
    The Feast of Tabernacles. 37

Chapter 9
    The Last Great Day. 41

Chapter 10
    Feast of Dedication or Hanukkah. 43

Chapter 11
    The Substance of the Feasts of the Lord. 47

Chapter 12
   Conclusion.....................................49

Preface

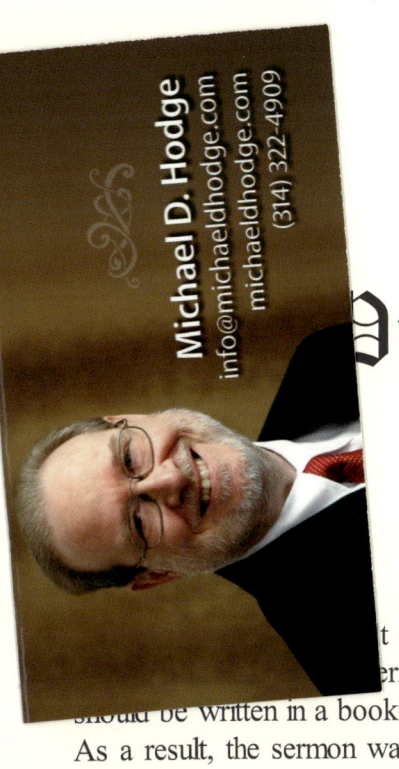

...t of a sermon which I gave in late 1979... ...ermon, it was suggested that the subject should be written in a booklet where it could be studied in depth. As a result, the sermon was transcribed from audio tape and the flow of the wording made easier to follow. It was originally printed in 1983.

From the start it was my desire to make some of the explanations more detailed, especially in the areas of the New Birth and the Feast of Trumpets. However, the Lord impressed upon me the importance of printing what I have and letting the reader do more private study and come to their own conclusions about what is presented.

I pray that the Lord will expand your vision to see all that He has for those who love Him and are the called according to His purpose which He purposed in Christ Jesus before the world began. (Romans 8:28; Ephesians 3:11 KJV)

God bless you as you grow in Him.

ii

Introduction

After the children of Israel were forcibly ejected from Egypt God led them through the wilderness to Mount Sinai where He revealed His laws to them. Among the revelations given at Mount Sinai is a series of Feasts or High Holy Days which are described in Leviticus Chapter 23:

> And the LORD spoke to Moses, saying, "Speak to the children of Israel, and say to them: 'The feasts of the LORD, which you shall proclaim *to be* holy convocations, these *are* My feasts.'" (Leviticus 23:1-2)

Please notice that these are not the "feasts of Moses." Moses did not give these feasts to the children of Israel. They are also not "Jewish feasts," but the Bible says they are the "The feasts of the LORD."

The purpose of this book is to discuss the meaning of God's feasts, not whether a Christian is required to keep the feasts today.

To some, the Holy Days are prophetic of things that will happen in the world around us. I don't see any problem with that kind of interpretation. We can see what has happened in the world historically and what is happening today as it relates to the Holy Days. Others understand the Holy Days in relationship to Church history revealing the sequence in which God is restoring truths previously lost to the church. In this approach each Holy Day represents a truth restored to common understanding. You see this by looking at the elementary or foundational principles and doctrines revealed in Hebrews 6:1-2.

What you'll read here is not intended to replace all other understanding you might have of the Holy Days. Some Christians believe, "Anything new I learn about the Bible and spiritual truth must replace all I previously knew on a particular subject." However, anything new we learn about the Bible does not have to replace what was previously known unless it totally contradicts and proves that what we believed before was in error. This leaves room for many "differing interpretations" of the same facts at the same time. The Bible can be understood on many different levels at the same time. Portions may apply spiritually and at the same time apply naturally. In fact, we learn more of the spiritual application of the scriptures if we understand the natural application. The apostle Paul put it this way:

> However, the spiritual is not first, but the natural, and afterward the spiritual. (1 Corinthians 15:46)

The Bible is a spiritual book, written to give us examples of how we should live. This is accomplished through giving us natural examples to guide us. 1 Corinthians 10:11, paraphrased, says, "The things that happened to Old Testament Israel were written as examples for us on whom the ends of the age have come." They are examples for us who have the spirit of God, so we can understand spiritual things.

One thing all interpretations of the Holy Days have in common is that they reveal God's plan for redeeming mankind. Throughout the Bible God uses various patterns to teach us. If we put certain patterns together with other patterns, we can gain a fuller understanding of what God is telling us. For example, the Tabernacle in the Wilderness contains a progression in the pieces of furniture that are within the Tabernacle as you move from the entrance of the outer court toward the Ark of the Covenant and the Mercy Seat. One day I took the various Holy Days and lined them up with the pieces of furniture in the Tabernacle. This comparison revealed more about the Holy Days from the things I knew about the Tabernacle, and I learned more about the Tabernacle from what I'd learned about the Holy Days. Another example is listing the elementary principles of Christ from Hebrews 6:1-2 mentioned earlier beside the Holy Days and the Tabernacle. By comparing patterns in this way, we can learn more about the meaning of each pattern. (See chart on page 11)

𝔘nto 𝔘s a 𝔗hild 𝔍s 𝔅orn will show us a comparison between the growth of an unborn child in the womb and the progression of the Holy Days from the beginning to the end of God's sacred calendar. This comparison also reveals an order in the spiritual growth of a Christian.

Do you know where you stand in your spiritual growth? Do you know what the next step should be in your normal growth? This study should give us at least a clue as to what our next step should be. We will be able to see whether or not we've even taken the first step in our spiritual development. Remember, though, that each person's growth is different. God deals with us individually and some things in our lives may happen out of what would be considered a "normal" sequence.

The rest of this book will contain quotes from Zola Levitt's book titled "THE SEVEN FEASTS OF ISRAEL." © Copyright 1979 by Zola Levitt (used by permission).

> Jesus answered, "Most assuredly, I say to you, unless one is born of water and the Spirit, he cannot enter the kingdom of God. That which is born of the flesh is flesh, and that which is born of the Spirit is spirit. Do not marvel that I said to you, 'You must be born again.' The wind blows where it wishes, and you hear the sound of it, but cannot tell where it comes from and where it goes. So is everyone who is born of the Spirit."

John 3:5-8

Chapter 1

The New Birth

Christians often talk about being "born again." They read the third chapter of John as saying that we have been born again. I believe, however, that Jesus was saying that each of us is pregnant — each of us is like a pregnant mother. The church is described as a woman. Paul wrote to the Corinthians:

> For though you might have ten thousand instructors in Christ, yet *you do* not *have* many fathers; for in Christ Jesus I have begotten you through the gospel. (1 Corinthians 4:15)

Paul also wrote to the Galatians:

> My little children, for whom I labor in birth again until Christ is formed in you, (Galatians 4:19)

The imagery is of a man who is having sympathy pains with his pregnant wife. Paul is saying, "Christ is being formed inside of you; He is growing up and some day He is going to come forth in completeness."

> I became a minister according to the stewardship from God which was given to me for you, to fulfill the word of God, the mystery which has been hidden from ages and from generations, but now has been revealed to His saints. To them God willed to make known what are the riches of the glory of this mystery among the Gentiles: which is Christ in you, the hope of glory. Him we preach, warning every man and teaching every man in all wisdom, that we may present every man perfect in Christ Jesus. (Colossians 1:25-28)

You see, it's Christ in you. We're all looking for glory, but it's Christ being formed in us that will bring about our glorification.

> Now a great sign appeared in heaven: **a woman clothed with the sun,** with the moon under her feet, and on her head a garland of twelve stars. (Revelation 12:1 Emphasis added)

One explanation of Revelation 12 says that the woman is the nation of Israel, who was married to God at Mount Sinai, and that Jesus is the child that is brought forth. But the child is described in verse 5:

> She bore a male Child who was to rule all nations with a rod of iron. And her Child was caught up to God and His throne. (Revelation 12:5)

Another explanation sees the woman as the bride of Christ, the bride being the Church. She will bring forth the child who is to rule all nations. Now, who is to rule all nations? Is it just Jesus?

The New Birth

Turning back to Revelation 2:26 we can find out what the Bible has to say about this.

> And he who overcomes, and keeps My works until the end, to him I will give power over the nations. (Revelation 2:26)

Jesus was saying this to believers. He is the King of kings, but a king doesn't administer a kingdom by himself. It is believers who are going to rule all nations with and under Him.

The child in Revelation 12 was a man-child (King James Version); a newborn, and yet he was a fully grown man. This is the same as when God created Adam. Adam was a complete, fully grown mature man, but he hadn't been brought forth into the world yet. God breathed into him the spirit of life and gave him life. In the same way, we will not come forth partly developed, but we're going to come forth fully mature beings. This relates to what Jesus said in John chapter three.

> Jesus answered, "Most assuredly, I say to you, unless one is born of water and the Spirit, he cannot enter the kingdom of God. That which is born of the flesh is flesh, and that which is born of the Spirit is spirit. Do not marvel that I said to you, 'You must be born again.'" (John 3:5-7)

Jesus is giving us an illustration of what He means by being born again. That which is born of the flesh is flesh. We have all been born of fleshly parents and are composed of flesh. When we have been born of the spirit we will be composed of spirit. He continues His illustration:

> "The wind blows where it wishes, and you hear the sound of it, but cannot tell where it comes from and where it goes. So is everyone who is born of the Spirit." (John 3:8)

A common explanation of John 3:8 is that being born of the Spirit happens mysteriously. You never know who the Spirit will blow upon next. But notice the words "*So is* everyone who is born of the Spirit." The phrase "so is" refers back to the description of the wind earlier in the verse. This verse could be stated this way: "Everyone who is born of the Spirit is like the wind which blows where it wishes, and you hear its sound, but cannot tell where it came from and where it is going."

Just like the wind, when you are fully born of the spirit, you will be able to do just as Jesus did after His resurrection. In John chapter twenty Jesus came into the midst of the disciples and they didn't know where He came from because the doors were locked. He didn't knock on the door; He just came and stood in their midst. This is the fullness of the new birth.

One thing I want to explain here is that this is translated out of the Greek language. In checking the New American Standard Bible, many places, especially in the book of 1 John where he talks about those that are born of God, you'll see a number and in the margin it says "begotten." The Greek word is Strong's #1080 *"gennao, ghen-nah'-o; from a variation of Greek #1085 (genos);* **to procreate (properly of the father***, but by extension of the mother); figurative to regenerate :- bear, beget, be born, bring forth, conceive, be delivered of, gender, make, spring."* Gennao means the whole birth process. It is used of begettal, the process of gestation, and of birth.

> having been born again [begotten again (Greek anagennao)], not of corruptible **seed** but incorruptible, through the word of God which lives and abides forever,
> (1 Peter 1:23 Emphasis added)

Now, you could very easily say that we are begotten again by the Word of God. It really makes no sense to say that a baby is born by the father's seed. The baby is begotten or conceived by the seed. Gennao is used this way in Matthew 1:20 when:

an angel of the Lord appeared to him in a dream, saying, "Joseph, son of David, do not be afraid to take to you Mary your wife, for that which is **conceived** in her is of the Holy Spirit." (Matthew 1:20 Emphasis added)

The father's seed brings conception. The mother carries the child to term and then it is born. The Word of God is the seed that fertilizes our egg, the human spirit, so we can begin growing spiritually. It is the Word of God that has the life in it and begets us. This interpretation is consistent with the Greek word "gennao" which includes the entire process from conception to parturition (or birth).

Yet there is a sense in which Christians are "born again" right now. 1 Peter 2:2 tells us to:

as **newborn** babes, desire the pure milk of the word, that you may grow thereby, (1 Peter 2:2)

To call a new Christian a "newborn" is a scriptural term. We are to act as newly born babes and start growing spiritually We must avoid getting hung up on semantics, striving about words (2 Timothy 2:14). However, we also need to know that the fullness of the new birth spoken of in the third chapter of John's gospel refers to something far beyond conversion.

The Seven Feasts of Israel

Now I'd like to quote from "The Seven Feasts of Israel" by Zola Levitt:

A most intriguing and startling application of the system of the seven feasts came my way recently during some research for a book.

I was asked by one of my publishers to look into writing a book about the birth of a baby from a biblical perspective. The book was to be a gift book to be presented to Christian couples at the arrival of blessed events.

I preferred to do more than just celebrate a new arrival; there are many adequate books for such purposes. Rather I wanted to find some theological principle, perhaps some hidden truth in the scriptures; about how each of us are born. I wanted to know if the scriptures held some secret as to how God makes us.

To that end I contacted Dr. Margaret Mathison, a Bible-reading friend, and a very good obstetrician who has delivered over ten thousand babies. (*"The Seven Feasts of Israel"* by Zola Levitt Page 19)

Behold what manner of love the Father has bestowed on us, that we should be called children of God! Therefore the world does not know us, because it did not know Him. Beloved, now we are children of God; and it has not yet been revealed what we shall be, but we know that when He is revealed, we shall be like Him, for we shall see Him as He is.

1 John 3:1-2

> On the fourteenth day of the first month at twilight is the LORD's Passover.

Leviticus 23:5

Chapter 2

Passover

It is really Margaret's first statement that turned me on to the whole system I'm about to disclose. I asked Margaret to tell me in some detail just how the baby is made and how it grows, and she began with this statement: "On the fourteenth day of the first month, the egg appears." I couldn't help hearing that familiar ring of Lev. 23:5: "In the fourteenth day of the first month . . .", God's original instruction of the observances of Passover. The Jews use an egg on the Passover table as symbolic of the new life they were granted by the sacrifice of the lamb in Egypt. (ibid Page 20)

Passover occurs on the fourteenth day of Abib, the first month of the Hebrew calendar (Leviticus 23:4-6). In Passover we receive the knowledge of God and of Jesus Christ and of His death. The beginning of our relationship with God is right here when God opens our minds to receive His seed. Let's look at Romans 10. Some of the scriptures in this chapter have been taken out of context and used to show some truths which are important to see, particularly verse seventeen which says: "So then faith *comes* by hearing, and hearing by the word of God." However, if you take verse seventeen in context, it's talking about a particular kind of faith and what that faith is for. Verse thirteen begins to allow us a little clue:

For *"whoever calls on the name of the* LORD *shall be saved."* (Romans 10:13)

The context shows here that Paul is talking about salvation.

How then shall they call on Him in whom they have not believed? And how shall they believe in Him of whom they have not heard? And how shall they hear without a preacher? And how shall they preach unless they are sent? As it is written:

"How beautiful are the feet of those who preach the gospel of peace, Who bring glad tidings of good things!"

But they have not all obeyed the gospel. For Isaiah says, *"Lord, who has believed our report?"* So then faith *comes* by hearing, and hearing by the word of God. (Romans 10:14-17)

We must all come to a place where we are prepared; the egg appears, and we're like that egg. We appear ready to accept the Word of God so that we can receive the faith necessary for salvation. In the woman's body, not every ovum matures and is ready for fertilization at the same time. Each person in the world comes to a place where he or she is ready to be impregnated; each is prepared at a different rate.

High Holy Day (Lev. 23)	Tabernacle Furniture	Foundational Teaching (Heb. 6:1-3)
Passover	Brazen Altar	Repentance from Dead Works
Unleavened Bread	Brazen Laver	Faith Toward God
Pentecost	Golden Lampstand	Baptisms
Trumpets	Table of Shewbread	Laying on of Hands
Atonement	Golden Altar of Incense	Resurrection of the Dead
Tabernacles	Ark of the Covenant	Eternal Judgment
Last Great Day	Mercy Seat	Going on to Perfection

Comparison Between
the Feasts of the Lord,
the Tabernacle Furniture and
the Doctrines of Hebrews 6 1-3

And on the fifteenth day of the same month is the Feast of Unleavened Bread to the LORD; seven days you must eat unleavened bread. On the first day you shall have a holy convocation; you shall do no customary work on it. But you shall offer an offering made by fire to the LORD for seven days. The seventh day shall be a holy convocation; you shall do no customary work on it.

Leviticus 23:6-8

Chapter 3

The Feast of Unleavened Bread

Now, let's read Mr. Levitt's description of the next thing that happens:

> I asked Margaret how soon fertilization of the mother's egg must occur if pregnancy is to happen. Her answer was very clear and very definite. "Fertilization must occur within twenty four hours, or the egg will pass on." (ibid Page 20)

The egg appears on the fourteenth day, and the fifteenth day of the first month is the first High Day of the Feast of Unleavened Bread (Leviticus 23:6-8). Fertilization, then has to take place quickly. Once we have come to the place where we are ready to receive salvation, it has to be brought in and received "or the egg will pass on." The Word has to be sent forth at the right time or it may not be accepted; fertilization has to take place at the right time. If it doesn't, it won't take place at all. Look at the parable of the sower in the fourth chapter of Mark.

> Listen! Behold, a sower went out to sow. (Mark 4:3)

The parable is given in verses four through nine and starting in verse fourteen Jesus gave the interpretation:

> "The sower sows the word. [*It's the Word of God that is sown.*] And these are the ones by the wayside where the word is sown. When they hear, Satan comes immediately and takes away the word that was sown in their hearts. These likewise are the ones sown on stony ground who, when they hear the word, immediately receive it with gladness; and they have no root in themselves, and so endure only for a time. Afterward, when tribulation or persecution arises for the word's sake, immediately they stumble. Now these are the ones sown among thorns; *they are* the ones who hear the word, and the cares of this world, the deceitfulness of riches, and the desires for other things entering in choke the word, and it becomes unfruitful. But these are the ones sown on good ground, those who hear the word, accept *it,* and bear fruit: some thirtyfold, some sixty, and some a hundred." (Mark 4:14-20)

Not everyone who hears the Word receives it and is fertilized. The sperm must enter the ovum for fertilization to take place. It must get past the hard shell, but when the DNA of the father joins with the DNA of the mother a *zygote* is formed which is the first, one celled form of human life. Once the egg is fertilized, if the next step does not happen, the zygote will die and be expelled from the mother's body. Some of those who receive the Word become spiritual miscarriages. Others go all the way, becoming fruitful members of Christ.

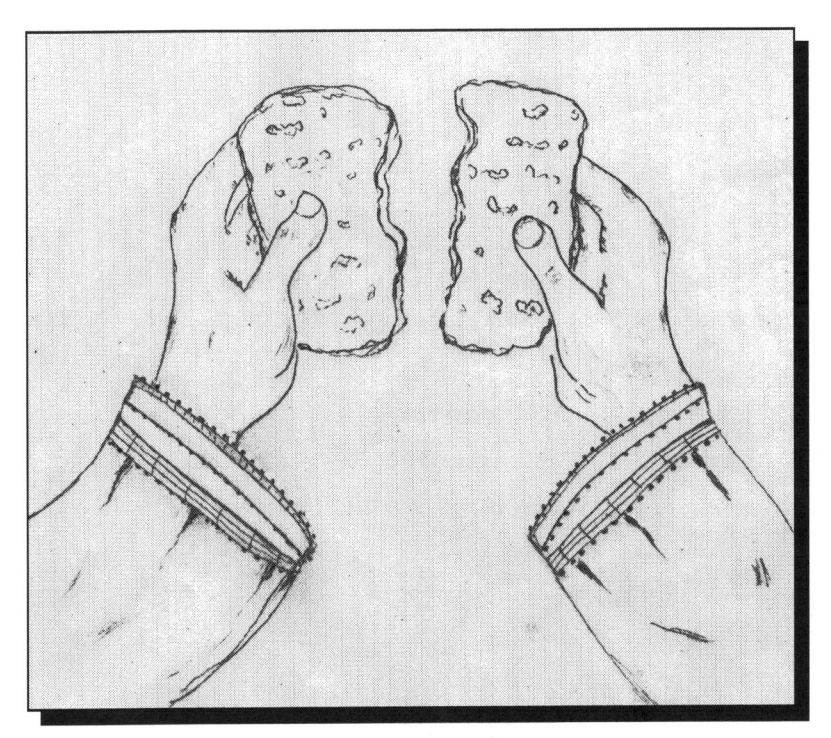

Unleavened Bread

Purge out therefore the old leaven, that ye may be a new lump, as ye are unleavened. For even Christ our passover is sacrificed for us:

1 Corinthians 5:7 (KJV)

And the LORD spoke to Moses, saying, "Speak to the children of Israel, and say to them: 'When you come into the land which I give to you, and reap its harvest, then you shall bring a sheaf of the firstfruits of your harvest to the priest. He shall wave the sheaf before the LORD, to be accepted on your behalf; on the day after the Sabbath the priest shall wave it. You shall eat neither bread nor parched grain nor fresh grain until the same day that you have brought an offering to your God; it shall be a statute forever throughout your generations in all your dwellings.'"

Leviticus 23:9-14

Chapter 4

The Wave Sheaf Offering

During the days of Unleavened Bread every year the priest would go into the tabernacle or the temple with what was called a wave sheaf (Leviticus 23:9-14). Mr. Levitt calls this activity First Fruits. What happened was that the people went out into the place where they were going to start reaping and they would take a sheaf of the firstfruits of the harvest and bring it to the priest who would wave it before God to be accepted for them. This marks the time from which the Feast of Pentecost is counted.

> I almost held my breath as I inquired about First Fruits. I realized that this third feast is not on a definite time cycle. It simply occurs on the Sunday during the week of Unleavened Bread. It could be the day after, or it could be almost a week away. I asked Margaret cautiously what happened next in the birth process.

"Well, that's a little bit indeterminate," she said. "The fertilized egg travels down the tube at its own speed toward the uterus. It may take anywhere from two to six days before it implants." (ibid Page 20-21)

The fertilized egg has to implant in the womb. This is where it receives its nourishment, from the mother through the umbilical cord. We have come into union with Christ.

But what does it say? *"The word is near you, in your mouth and in your heart"* (that is, the word of faith which we preach): that if you confess with your mouth the Lord Jesus and believe in your heart that God has raised Him from the dead, you will be saved. For with the heart one believes unto righteousness, and with the mouth confession is made unto salvation. (Romans 10:8-10)

It's in the heart. In other words, the word of faith goes out and gets into your heart. Remember, what Jesus said about the heart?

"out of the abundance of the heart the mouth speaks." (Matthew 12:34b)

It is in your heart that the Word is planted and it is in your mouth that it is spoken to become effective by confessing that Jesus Christ is the Lord of your life. So once you have heard the word, you receive it, act upon it and it goes down and implants into the very center of your being — in your heart.

Jesus is alive and living and He wants to come and live within us. We have to be grafted in to the mother, or to the source of our life, so that we can begin to grow. If we don't get grafted in, we're never going to be able to grow. We may have received the fertilizing, but never been grafted in.

"I am the vine, you *are* the branches. He who abides in Me, and I in him, bears much fruit; for without Me you can do nothing. If anyone does not abide in Me, he is cast out as a branch and is withered; and they gather them and throw *them* into the fire, and they are burned." (John 15:5-6)

If the egg doesn't get grafted in, there's a menstruation and the whole thing is flushed out of the woman's body and the process has to start all over again. As an example, my wife and I went through an experience some years ago with a sister-in-law. She attended a meeting ready to receive. When we brought her home she was talking about how much she was touched, but we didn't really know how to help her get grafted in where she needed to be. So then, the whole process had to start over; and she went through some real problems. The Old Testament says that a woman that is in her period is unclean. If you see someone who's been through this process, you're not to touch them spiritually because you can damage them. It's not the right time. Whenever it's God's time, they will be brought back. It's similar to the monthly cycle in a woman. They don't have just one chance; God will continue to lead them and draw them to Himself in His own time.

On the day of the wave sheaf offering, after Jesus had been resurrected, Mary went to the tomb and saw Him. Then Jesus said:

> "**Touch me not**; for I am not yet ascended to my Father: but go to my brethren, and say unto them, I ascend unto my Father, and your Father; and *to* my God, and your God." (John 20:17 KJV Emphasis added)

Some newer versions such as the New King James translate Jesus's words as "Do not cling to me." This is an erroneous translation. The Greek word is Strong's #680 (haptomai). Every other time it appears in the New Testament it is translated "touch" and means to touch as in the incident where Jesus was touched by the woman with the issue of blood (Luke 8:42-44). Jesus would not let Mary touch Him because He had not yet been accepted by the Father as the Wave Sheaf Offering. The same day (the day of

First Fruits) Jesus came back and his disciples were not restricted from touching Him. He fulfilled the wave sheaf offering by going to the Father and being accepted as the first of the firstfruits. He was the first of the firstfruits, accepted by the Father, so that the rest of us who are the firstfruits can be brought in.

> Then, the same day at evening, being the first *day* of the week, when the doors were shut where the disciples were assembled, for fear of the Jews, Jesus came and stood in the midst, and said to them, "Peace *be* with you." When He had said this, He showed them *His* hands and His side. Then the disciples were glad when they saw the Lord. So Jesus said to them again, "Peace to you! As the Father has sent Me, I also send you." And when He had said this, He breathed on *them,* and said to them, "Receive the Holy Spirit. If you forgive the sins of any, they are forgiven them; if you retain the *sins* of any, they are retained." (John 20:19-23)

Jesus gave them the Holy Spirit. Right then, they were begotten. They were grafted in on that wave sheaf day. The disciples had been brought along and they were ready, and He grafted them into Himself on that day. The baptism in the Holy Spirit had not yet been given because Jesus had not yet been glorified, but now He was ready to bring them into the next stage.

Wave Sheaf Offering

Jesus saith unto her, Touch me not; for I am not yet ascended to my Father: but go to my brethren, and say unto them, I ascend unto my Father, and your Father; and to my God, and your God.

John 20:17 (KJV)

And you shall count for yourselves from the day after the Sabbath, from the day that you brought the sheaf of the wave offering: seven Sabbaths shall be completed. Count fifty days to the day after the seventh Sabbath; then you shall offer a new grain offering to the LORD. ... And you shall proclaim on the same day that it is a holy convocation to you. You shall do no customary work on it. It shall be a statute forever in all your dwellings throughout your generations.

Leviticus 23:15-16, 21

Chapter 5

Pentecost

Seven weeks plus one day (or fifty days) from the Wave Sheaf Offering is the Feast of Pentecost also known as the Feast of Weeks (Leviticus 23:15-22).

I asked Margaret cautiously what the next development would be with our implanted egg.

"Well, of course, we have a slowly developing embryo here for a long time," she said. "It goes through stages, but there is no really dramatic change until it becomes an actual fetus. That's the big event." And she turned her medical book toward me so that I could see a page divided like a calendar, showing the first few weeks of the embryonic development.

I looked across the little pictures at what seemed like a little tadpole, which soon had flippers, and then began to look like a little man from Mars, and so on, down to the very last picture on the page. There I saw a human baby, and beside that drawing the very Scriptural message, "fifty days."

I looked up at Margaret, trying to conceal my excitement, and said carefully, "Is the fiftieth day important?"

"Well," said the obstetrician, "Up until the fiftieth day, you wouldn't know if you're going to have a duck or a cocker spaniel. But at the fiftieth day of the embryo, it becomes a human fetus." (ibid Page 21-22)

Once the egg and sperm have united at the Feast of Unleavened Bread, the DNA of a new human child being created by joining DNA from the mother and father, **there is never a question about what the end result will be.** The DNA contains the genetic blueprint which determines the life form into which the cells will develop. In the same way, once the Spirit of God joins with a human spirit, a new child of God is begotten. Just as the human embryo may not **appear to the naked eye** to be human, a newly begotten Christian may not **appear to the world** to be a child of God for some time. That, however, does not change the underlying DNA, and the fact that a human child will be born having characteristics of both parents. Notice what the Apostle John had to say:

> Beloved, we are [even here and] now God's children; it is not yet disclosed (made clear) what we shall be [hereafter], but we know that when He comes and is manifested, we shall [as God's children] resemble and be like Him, for we shall see Him just as He [really] is. (1 John 3:2 AMP)

The child becomes recognizable as a human baby on the fiftieth day. What happened to the Church on the day of Pentecost? It received the baptism in the Holy Spirit, but it also took on a structure you could recognize. It began to be recognized by the rest of the world as the Church of God.

There is going to come a time in your life and in my life when the world looks at us, and they'll say, "... there's something different about them." We're now different. We become recognizable as a child of God. What does the Bible say it is that makes us recognizable?

> For as many as are led by the Spirit of God, these are sons of God. (Romans 8:14)

We'll be recognizable as children of God when we are led by the Spirit of God, and not by the spirit of man or our own human spirit, or by something else. How will the Spirit of God, the Holy Spirit, lead us?

> Now hope does not disappoint, because the love of God has been poured out in our hearts by the Holy Spirit who was given to us. (Romans 5:5)

We'll be recognizable because the Holy Spirit will shed abroad the love of God.

> "By this all will know that you are My disciples, if you have love for one another." (John 13:35)

Christians are not recognizable by the fact that they go to Church every week. We're not recognized by a particular doctrinal belief. It's not because we're a member of a particular organization. God's love demonstrated through us marks us as true children of God.

> For God has not given us a spirit of fear, but of power and of love and of a sound mind. (2 Timothy 1:7)

We receive that power and love through the Holy Spirit, and Pentecost.

Then the LORD spoke to Moses, saying, "Speak to the children of Israel, saying: 'In the seventh month, on the first day of the month, you shall have a sabbath-rest, a memorial of blowing of trumpets, a holy convocation. You shall do no customary work on it; and you shall offer an offering made by fire to the LORD.'"

Leviticus 23:23-25

Chapter 6

The Feast of Trumpets

After Pentecost, there's a long period of time until the Feast of Trumpets, which is the first day of the seventh month (Leviticus 23:23-25).

> I next asked Margaret about the first day of the seventh month. I had hoped that there were no big events through what would be a long summer on the schedule of the feasts, and indeed there were none. The perfection that arrived just at the beginning of the seventh month, was the baby's hearing. At the first day of the seventh month, the baby could discriminate a sound for what it really was. For example, a trumpet was a trumpet! (ibid Page 22-23)

In John 10 Jesus addressed the importance of hearing God's voice.

> "Most assuredly, I say to you, he who does not enter the sheepfold by the door, but climbs up some other way, the same is a thief and a robber. But he who enters by the door is the shepherd of the sheep. To him the doorkeeper opens, and the sheep hear his voice; and he calls his own sheep by name and leads them out." (John 10:1-3)

The shepherds took their sheep in at night, letting them intermingle. In the morning, the doorkeeper would open the door to the shepherd. He would open it to no one else. Then the shepherd went in and called. The sheep recognized their own shepherd's voice and went to him. As believers, we must learn to recognize and follow only the voice of our Shepherd, Jesus Christ.

> "And when he brings out his own sheep, he goes before them; and the sheep follow him, for they know his voice. Yet they will by no means follow a stranger, but will flee from him, for they do not know the voice of strangers." (John 10:4-5)

We can't be led by the Spirit of God without really hearing God's voice. There are several ways that God speaks to His people. These include the "still small voice" within, the audible voice of the Lord, visions, and dreams. We shall all have spiritual hearing.

When the people arrived at Mt. Sinai, God told Moses to speak to the children of Israel saying:

> Now therefore, if you will indeed obey My voice and keep My covenant, then you shall be a special treasure to Me above all people; for all the earth *is* Mine. And you shall be to Me a kingdom of priests and a holy nation. (Exodus 19:5-6)

God told them that He wanted them to "obey my voice." In Exodus 19:16-25 God showed up to talk to the people. The whole mountain was shaking, and smoking, and God's voice was described as a trumpet. Exodus 20:18-19 says that the people didn't want to have God speak to them. They were frightened of Him. From that time on, the people had to depend upon Moses, or one of the prophets, or a priest to tell them what God said. However, God's sons are to be attentive to His voice, and to be "led by the Spirit of God."

Through Bible study and obedience to God's word, we develop an ability to distinguish the voice of God from other voices. God speaks from His Temple through the priesthood. In the Old Testament when a person wanted to hear from God, he went to God's Temple. Where is God's temple today? You are the Temple of God (1 Corinthians 3:17)! God still speaks to His priesthood. Who is His priesthood?

> But you *are* a chosen generation, a royal priesthood, a holy nation, His own special people, that you may proclaim the praises of Him who called you out of darkness into His marvelous light (1 Peter 2:9)

The church is the priesthood God speaks to. We must each grow spiritually to the point that we can hear God's voice for ourselves. Then we will know that we are doing what He wants. We must develop our spiritual hearing.

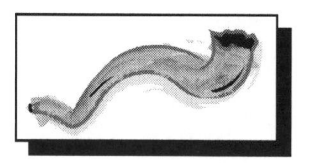

Feast of Trumpets

And the LORD spoke to Moses, saying: "Also the tenth day of this seventh month shall be the Day of Atonement. It shall be a holy convocation for you; you shall afflict your souls, and offer an offering made by fire to the LORD. And you shall do no work on that same day, for it is the Day of Atonement, to make atonement for you before the LORD your God. For any person who is not afflicted in soul on that same day shall be cut off from his people. And any person who does any work on that same day, that person I will destroy from among his people. You shall do no manner of work; it shall be a statute forever throughout your generations in all your dwellings. It shall be to you a sabbath of solemn rest, and you shall afflict your souls; on the ninth day of the month at evening, from evening to evening, you shall celebrate your sabbath."

Leviticus 23:26-32

Chapter 7

The Day of Atonement

Following the Feast of Trumpets is a ten day period followed by the Day of Atonement (Leviticus 23:26-32). The whole sixteenth chapter of Leviticus is devoted to the instructions for the Day of Atonement. It consisted of two parts. The first had to do with the High Priest entering into the Holiest Place with the blood of a goat to sprinkle on the Mercy Seat. This process made atonement for the sins of Israel until the next Day of Atonement. The second instruction was that all the people were to fast, not eating anything from sunset to sunset. Let's notice what Mr. Levitt has to say about the Day of Atonement:

> Half quoting from her textbook and concentrating hard, Margaret stated that the important changes now . . . were in the blood. It was necessary for the fetal blood, which carried the mother's oxygen through the baby's system, to change in such a way that the baby could carry the oxygen

that it, itself, would obtain upon birth. Technically, the hemoglobin of the blood would have to change from that of the fetus to that of a self-respirating and circulating human being. The fetus does not breathe, but rather depends on the oxygen obtained through the mother's blood circulation. Naturally, this system must be changed before birth and that change occurs, according to Margaret's textbook, in the second week of the seventh month, to be precise, on the tenth day! (ibid Page 23)

In the Old Testament we are instructed not to eat blood (Leviticus 3:17) but we are to pour out the blood. The life of the flesh is shown to be in the blood. But Jesus made a very interesting statement in John 6 about our life. We have been looking at the flesh as being our life, but Jesus is saying to us:

> It is the Spirit who gives life; the flesh profits nothing. The words that I speak to you are spirit, and *they* are life. (John 6:63)

At the Day of Atonement we recognize that life does not originate in our flesh. Realizing that fact causes a transformation in how we view the source of our life. Our life is not in our flesh; it's in our spirit (James 2:26). Eternal life comes from the Spirit of God dwelling in our spirit.

> "A little while longer and the world will see Me no more, but you will see Me. Because I live, you will live also. At that day you will know that I *am* in My Father, and you in Me, and I in you." (John 14:19-20)

At that day you shall *know* that I am in the Father, and you're in me and I in you. We're all together, you see. The Day of Atonement shows oneness (at-one-ment) with God. Through being joined to Christ Jesus we are one spirit with God now (1 Corinthians 6:17). However, there's coming a time, Jesus said, when we would ***know*** it. We have the seed of Christ in us. Christ

The Day of Atonement

is being formed within us (Galatians 4:19). We must decrease, but He must increase until He fills our whole being. Now we are one with Christ in spirit, but we don't *know* it yet in our minds which are a part of our souls. There will come a time when union with Christ will move from our spirits to our souls, to our minds, and we'll know with an undeniable knowledge. The Day of Atonement shows us that time. In Jesus's prayer in John 17:21, He said:

> "that they all may be one, as You, Father, *are* in Me, and I in You; that they also may be one in Us, that the world may believe that You sent Me." (John 17:21)

Our unity is not in each other; it is in Christ; it's in the Father. We are to be one with God the same way Jesus is one with the Father.

> He who has the Son has life; he who does not have the Son of God does not have life. (1 John 5:12)

> But he who is joined to the Lord is one spirit *with Him*. (1 Corinthians 6:17)

Those are simple statements. We are one spirit with Christ. It is our spirit. It is the spirit that gives life. When we stop looking at outward things for eternal life and begin looking to the Spirit of God within, we will *know* that we are one with the Father and that we *have* eternal life!

> For the mind set on the flesh is death, but the mind set on the Spirit is life and peace, (Romans 8:6 NASB)

It's in the mind. If your mind is thinking about the flesh all the time, it brings death; if your mind is set on the spirit, it brings life. Atonement is the Fast. It shows us that our life is not really dependent upon natural things. The unborn child is dependent upon its physical connection to the mother for life. However, the time comes when there is no need for that connection to continue. In spiritual growth we come to the place where we say with Paul:

> I am crucified with Christ: nevertheless I live; yet not I, but Christ liveth in me: and the life which I now live in the flesh I live by the faith of the Son of God, who loved me, and gave himself for me. (Galatians 2:20 KJV)

The Day of Atonement is when this scripture is going to be fulfilled and we'll have its full meaning in our lives. We are going to **know** we have been crucified and that Christ is now our life (Colossians 3:4).

The body without the spirit is dead

James 2:26

Then the LORD spoke to Moses, saying, "Speak to the children of Israel, saying: 'The fifteenth day of this seventh month shall be the Feast of Tabernacles for seven days to the LORD. On the first day there shall be a holy convocation. You shall do no customary work on it.'"

Leviticus 23:33-35

Chapter 8

The Feast of Tabernacles

On the fifteenth day of the seventh month is the Feast of Tabernacles (Leviticus 23:33-36). Let me explain something to you about the Feast of Tabernacles, because every book I've ever read except a very few miss one point in the description of this feast in Leviticus.

> Also on the fifteenth day of the seventh month, when you have gathered in the fruit of the land, you shall keep the feast of the LORD *for* seven days; on the first day *there shall be* a sabbath-*rest,* and on the eighth day a sabbath-rest. (Leviticus 23:39)

There is a separate Feast attached to the end of the Feast of Tabernacles. The Feast of Tabernacles is seven days. The first and eighth days are Sabbaths or High Days. Since the Feast of Tabernacles is only seven days, this eighth day must be (technically) a separate feast. We'll have more to say about that in the next chapter, but on the fifteenth day of the seventh month something else happens.

> I asked for the fifteenth day of the seventh month, and she immediately recognized the date as the beginning of the safe delivery period. "You see, that's when the lungs are developed," she said, "and as long as they get their little lungs going, we can bring them along, even if they are born at that early time. I'm afraid if they decide to come before those lungs are finished, then they have little chance. But by the fifteenth day of the seventh month, a normal baby has two healthy lungs, and if born at that point, can take in its own air and live on it." (ibid Page 23-24)

We've developed a knowledge that the spirit is our life, but there's something else. There will be a time when our spiritual lungs will have developed. We will no longer be dependent upon a connection to the physical world for life just as the unborn child is no longer dependent upon the umbilical cord for life once the lungs have developed.

> And so it is written, *"The first man Adam became a living being."* The last Adam *became* a life-giving spirit. (1 Corinthians 15:45)

God breathed physical breath into the first Adam and he became a physical being— a soulish being. But God wants to breathe into us the Spirit of Life so that we can exist outside our physical world in the spiritual world. Remember Jesus going to heaven following His resurrection on the Wave Sheaf day? He moved from this physical world to the spirit world where the Father is. There was no physical air there. What did He breathe? He breathed the spiritual air.

Feast of Tabernacles

And the Word became flesh and dwelt (tabernacled) among us, and we beheld His glory, the glory as of the only begotten of the Father, full of grace and truth.

John 1:14

Also on the fifteenth day of the seventh month, when you have gathered in the fruit of the land, you shall keep the feast of the LORD for seven days; on the first day there shall be a sabbath-rest, and on the eighth day a sabbath-rest.

Leviticus 23:39

Chapter 9

The Last Great Day

The Last Great Day is the twenty second day of the seventh month (Leviticus 23:39) and is not covered in Mr. Zola Levitt's book, but I saw something in John the seventh chapter concerning this Feast when Jesus went up to Jerusalem to keep the Feast of Tabernacles.

> On the last day, that great *day* of the feast [*this is why it is called The Last Great Day*], Jesus stood and cried out, saying, "If anyone thirsts, let him come to Me and drink. He who believes in Me, as the Scripture has said, out of his heart will flow rivers of living water." But this He spoke concerning the Spirit, whom those believing in Him would receive; for the Holy Spirit was not yet *given,* because Jesus was not yet glorified. (John 7:37-39)

This will come welling up out of us; it's going to start having an effect on others; the Spirit in us affecting others. This will be, as it says, ". . . A **river** of living water," a **river** of life. We really do have a river down inside of us. I'm afraid some of us have put a tap on it and we've shut the tap off. But when it starts flowing like a river, we won't be able to put a tap on it. You can't put a tap on the Mississippi River. It just flows around your tap. And we're going to come to a place where that happens in us also.

Chapter 10

Feast of Dedication or Hanukkah

On the fifteenth day of the seventh month, the lungs are developed. From that day forward, the baby could be delivered and live. Everything is ready for birth. But that is only approximately two hundred days. What about the two hundred and eighty days it takes for the full gestation of a human child? Remember, the Feast of Tabernacles (which includes The Last Great Day), is "the end of the road," the end of the feasts. The baby would live if born at the Feast of Tabernacles, but there are another eighty days before the normal baby finally leaves its dwelling place of darkness and enters into the light — a total of two hundred and eighty days!

Following the system, then, to the two hundred and eightieth day of the Hebrew calendar we come, right on schedule, to the Feast of Dedication. The Feast of Dedication, or Hanukkah (also spelled Chanukah), as it is called today, was not given by God at Mount Sinai, but it does, nevertheless, seem to have a divine origin. John 10:22 says that Jesus Himself observed the Feast of Dedication.

According to Falvious Josephus, a Jewish historian who lived in the first century, Hanukkah was the result of a prophecy given by Daniel. According to Daniel 8:9-14, the Abomination of Desolation would result in the daily sacrifice at the temple being taken away. Then, after 2300 days, the sanctuary would be cleansed. This prophecy was fulfilled, (according to Antiquities of the Jews, Book xii, chapter vii, paragraphs 6-7) about 170 years before Christ was born. It was then that Antiochus Epiphanes, a Syrian general, brought his army against the city of Jerusalem and waged war for three and a half years, finally capturing the Temple Mount. He desecrated the Temple by sacrificing a sow upon the altar. Josephus said this was the Abomination of Desolation spoken of by Daniel the Prophet. Zola Levitt has this to say about Chanukah:

> The nature of Chanukah has to do with the eternal light in the Temple (and in every synagogue today). God had made a great miracle on the occasion when Antiochus entered the Temple and sacrificed a sow on the altar. The Macabees threw him out but found only one precious can of consecrated oil — a day's supply — with which to maintain the eternal light. A great miracle answered their prayers, however. The oil lasted eight days and sustained the light until more was ready. And so the Jews will light a candle each night for eight nights on the Feast of Chanukah.
>
> I found what I fully expected on the Jewish calendar. Chanukah lies just the right distance beyond Tabernacles to account for the actual birth of the baby. (ibid Page 24-25)

In Paul's first letter to the Corinthians, he was answering questions that the people of Corinth had brought to him. One of

Feast of Dedication or Hanukkah

which was about the resurrection and what kind of body those in the resurrection would have. Paul answered them this way:

> All flesh *is* not the same flesh, but *there is* one *kind of* flesh of men, another flesh of animals, another of fish, *and* another of birds. *There are* also celestial bodies and terrestrial bodies; but the glory of the celestial *is* one, and the *glory* of the terrestrial *is* another. *There is* one glory of the sun, another glory of the moon, and another glory of the stars; for *one* star differs from *another* star in glory. So also *is* the resurrection of the dead. *The body* is sown in corruption, it is raised in incorruption. (1 Corinthians 15:39-42)

We'll be raised with glory; an eternal light shining out sustained by Christ in us. We'll be able to see wherever we go because we'll carry His light with us. Some of us will shine like the sun, so bright you just can't look. Others will shine like the moon with lesser glory. There will be as many different kinds of glory as there are stars in the night sky.

> Then Jesus spoke to them again, saying, "I am the light of the world. He who follows Me shall not walk in darkness, but have the light of life." (John 8:12)

We can walk in that light right now but we're going to have the Light of Life not just with us, but in us, emanating from us. It's very interesting that James says:

> Every good gift and every perfect gift is from above, and comes down from the Father of lights. (James 1:17)

Isn't that interesting? He says God is the Father of *lights*. It's interesting too, how this whole Feast deals with light. We have been positionally translated from a realm of darkness to a realm of light, but we're still walking in that realm of darkness. We're in the physical world and the darkness is all around us. The baby comes out of the mother's womb, from a world of darkness, into a world of light. If you think you've been living in light— just wait! There is coming a day when we'll be born again from this world into a world of light.

Chapter 11

The Substance of the Feasts of the Lord

So let no one judge you in food or in drink, or regarding a festival or a new moon or sabbaths, which are a shadow of things to come, but the substance (body - KJV) is of Christ. (Colossians 2:16-17)

The King James version of this verse has the word "is" in *italics*, indicating that the translators added it to help make the original thought clear. This is the correct translation even though some people would take the word "is" out of the verse to make the sense of the verse be that "you're not to let any man judge you about the holy days but let the body of Christ judge you." In effect this makes the verse say "don't let any man judge you, but let me (a church leader — a man) judge you."

The subject Paul is discussing is the substance that is casting the shadows. A shadow is a spot of darkness in the form and shape of the substance which is blocking light. But if you want to find out what is casting the shadow, you have to take your eyes off of the shadow, and look back to where the light is. Then you'll see what's casting the shadow. Better translations of this verse state it this way:

> "which are a shadow of things to come, but the substance is Christ."

The substance that casts the shadows of the Holy Days, of the Sabbath days, and of all that Israel went through, is Christ. We're brought right back again to Christ. The ultimate fulfillment of all the Holy Days and the Sabbaths is Christ in you.

Chapter 12

Conclusion

I ask you again, do you know where you are in your spiritual growth? Each of us will be in different places in this pattern. Some of us haven't even made the first step. If that is the case, now may be your time to receive that initial begettal by repenting of your sins and confessing Jesus Christ as Lord, then asking the Father to give you the Holy Spirit.

> For the Scripture says, *"Whoever believes on Him will not be put to shame."* For there is no distinction between Jew and Greek, for the same Lord over all is rich to all who call upon Him. For *"whoever calls on the name of the LORD shall be saved."* (Romans 10:11-13)

Some of us have grown to where we can begin keeping the Feast of Trumpets, hearing God instruct us daily what it is that He wants us to do.

Conclusion

> Therefore, my beloved, as you have always obeyed, not as in my presence only, but now much more in my absence, work out your own salvation with fear and trembling; for it is God who works in you both to will and to do for *His* good pleasure. (Philippians 2:12-13)

We have a part in making sure that we reach the next step in these spiritual growth patterns, but it is Christ in us. The scripture says, "for it is God which works in you . . ." It is not we ourselves doing it, but we have to work it out, allowing God to work out through us the spiritual growth.

If we expect to come to the place where we hear God's voice, where we know that our life is not from the flesh but from the spirit, we're going to have to spend some time with God drawing in spiritual nourishment through our spiritual umbilical cord. We're going to have to work out our salvation. Yet, I want to caution you. Don't go overboard in that because you've been grafted into the vine. You can't of yourself produce fruit. It's Christ in you producing the fruit. The unborn child does not work hard to grow in the womb. It just gets attached to the source of life and stays attached. Growth results. And I just say, let's get attached to Christ and rest in Him. Then we'll start growing, and growing.

I want to encourage you, then, not to look at the Holy Days as just physical days to be observed, not to look at the Holy Days just as something that is going to happen in the world that we're all going to stand back and watch. Understand that the Feasts of the Lord have a spiritual meaning and rejoice in the Feasts — rejoice and worship God in spirit and truth, for God seeks such to worship Him.

Contact the Author

Email: info@michaeldhodge.com

Web Site: www.michaeldhodge.com

Other Books by Michael D. Hodge

Where is the United States in Bible Prophecy?

Made in the USA
Charleston, SC
04 October 2012